here is only one success

To be able to spend your life

ur own way.

RISTOPHER MORLEY

ALSO BY BARBARA MILO OHRBACH

IF YOU THINK YOU CAN...

YOU CAN!

BY BARBARA MILO OHRBACH

CLARKSON POTTER/PUBLISHERS NEW YORK

Published by Clarkson N. Potter/Publishers, 201 East 50th Street,
New York, New York 10022.
Member of the Crown Publishing Group.

Random House, Inc. New York, Toronto,
London, Sydney, Auckland

www.randomhouse.com

CLARKSON N. POTTER, POTTER and colophon
are trademarks of Clarkson N. Potter, Inc.

Printed in the United States of America
Design by Dania Martinez Davey

Library of Congress Cataloging-in-Publication Data
Ohrbach, Barbara Milo.
If you think you can . . . you can! / by Barbara Milo Ohrbach. —
1st ed.
1. Quotations, English. 2. Quotations. I. Title.
PN6081.047   1998
082—dc21   97-44530
CIP

ISBN 0-609-80317-4
10 9 8 7 6 5 4 3

ACKNOWLEDGMENTS

Where would any of us be without all the people who have encouraged us along the way? Often, they're the ones who realize that we can do it <u>before</u> we do!

I've been very lucky to have had many mentors in my life. I can see their faces now, and how I wish I could personally thank each one of them for their caring and guidance: Mavis C. Bingley, Charles Burge, Annette David, Rudy Ferrari, Bess Ficks, Nanette Frand, Barbara Lolly, Jane Marshall, DeMares O'Connell, Lee Ohrbach, Richard Ohrbach, Helen Rhodes, William Ruben, Norma Sams, Mildred L. Smith, Margaret Spicer-Simpson. And of course, Mom and Dad, Grandma Annette, Grandpa Thomas, and my husband, Mel.

Special thanks to Deborah Geltman, Gayle Benderoff, Annetta Hanna, and Dania Martinez Davey for all their good, good work, and all my friends at Clarkson Potter: Mary Ellen Briggs, Joan Denman, Chip Gibson, Andrea Peabbles, Marysarah Quinn, Wendy Schuman, Lauren Shakely, John Son, Robin Strashun, and Jane Treuhaft. And especially to Gail Shanks, who always generously and graciously did more than her share—thank you.

ou must do the things that you cannot do—
you gain strength, courage, and confidence
by every experience in which you really stop
to look fear in the face.

Eleanor Roosevelt made this statement as she was
facing one of the many obstacles in a life filled with
wonderful accomplishments.

We all face obstacles in our lives, but today pessimism
seems to surround us. By limiting expectations, we may
protect ourselves from failure, possible embarrassment,
and disappointment. But if one expects little or nothing,
that's what one often ends up with. In the end it's
a self-fulfilling prophecy.

Optimism, on the other hand, can also be a self-
fulfilling prophecy—one that fills us with elation,
strength, and a sense of accomplishment. It is easier not

making the effort or taking the risks, but if we don't believe in ourselves, we may miss the wonderful opportunities, possibilities, and joys that life holds for us.

There *are* obstacles to almost anything. Once we realize that they can be overcome, we start to grow. I think that we should all try to ...

- Be *realistically* optimistic.
- Set reachable goals and not compare ourselves with the person who just won the lottery or invented computers.
- Associate with positive people. Kindred spirits help us believe in ourselves and engender hope.
- Have the courage of our convictions. Negative attitudes will do us in.

And last, but not least, let optimism work to make our dreams come true. I just read that life is like an echo—we get from it what we put into it, and often much more!

—BARBARA MILO OHRBACH

Light

This Book Graciously Donated By
Deirdre Kettlewell

tomorrow
with
to-day!

ELIZABETH BARRETT BROWNING

Live contented.

PAUL REVERE

Some day you will find out that there is
far more happiness in another's happiness
than in your own.
It is something I cannot explain,
something within that sends
a glow of warmth all through you.

HONORÉ DE BALZAC

Always laugh when you can. It is cheap medicine.

LORD BYRON

I believe in the possibility of *happiness*.

GEORGE SANTAYANA

We should consider every day lost on
which we have not danced at least once.

FRIEDRICH WILHELM NIETZSCHE

Try as much as possible to be wholly alive,
with all your might, and when you laugh,
laugh like hell and when you get angry,
get good and angry. Try to be alive.
You will be dead soon enough.

WILLIAM SAROYAN

However mean your life is, meet it and live it;
do not shun and call it hard names.
It is not so bad as you are. It looks poorest
when you are richest.... *Love your life*.

HENRY DAVID THOREAU

Our goal should be to achieve joy.

LEO CASTILLO

That which you vividly imagine,
sincerely believe, ardently desire and
enthusiastically act upon will inevitably come to pass.

WILLIAM R. LUCAS

When you say *"I will"* with conviction,
magic begins to happen.

WALLY AMOS

Enthusiasm is
the greatest asset
in the world.
It beats money and
power and influence.

HENRY CHESTER

Throw your heart over the fence
and the rest will follow.

NORMAN VINCENT PEALE

12

Discover what you want most of all
in this world, and set yourself to work on it.

JOHN HOMER MILLER

The toughest thing about success is that
you've got to keep on being a success.
Talent is only a starting point in this business.
You've got to keep on working that talent.

IRVING BERLIN

Be not afraid of growing slowly,
Be afraid only of standing still.

CHINESE PROVERB

When you are not practicing, remember,
someone somewhere is practicing, and
when you meet him he will win.

ED MACAULEY

Practice what you know, and it will help to make
clear what now you do not know.

REMBRANDT

You may be whatever you resolve to be.
Determine to be something in the world,
and you will be something.
"I cannot" never accomplished anything;
"I will try" has wrought wonders.

JOEL HAWES

*A*bove all things,
reverence yourself.

PYTHAGORAS

Go to your bosom;
Knock there, and ask your heart what it doth know.

WILLIAM SHAKESPEARE

Guard well within yourself that treasure, kindness.
Know how to give without hesitation,
how to lose without regret,
how to acquire without meanness.

GEORGE SAND

If you want to be respected,
you must respect yourself.

SPANISH PROVERB

Believe in yourself!
Have faith in your abilities!

NORMAN VINCENT PEALE

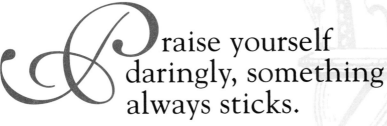

raise yourself
daringly, something
always sticks.

FRANCIS BACON

I always knew I wanted to be somebody.
I think that's where it begins. People decide,
"I want to be somebody. I want to make a
contribution. I want to leave my mark here."
Then different factors contribute
to how you will do that.

FAITH RINGGOLD

Ah, but a
should exce

Or what's a

man's reach

ed his grasp,

heaven for?

ROBERT BROWNING

Live all you can; it's a mistake not to.

HENRY JAMES

Carpe diem, Seize the day . . .

HORACE

*B*e not afraid of life.
Believe that life
is worth living, and
your belief will help
create the fact.

WILLIAM JAMES

I'm passionately involved in life:
I love its change, its color, its movement.
To be alive, to be able to see, to walk,
to have houses, music, paintings—
it's all a miracle.

ARTHUR RUBINSTEIN

All life is an experiment.
The more experiments you make, the better.

RALPH WALDO EMERSON

One way to get
the most out of
life is to look upon it
as an adventure.

WILLIAM FEATHER

I have alway felt that the moment
when first you wake up in the morning
is the most wonderful of the 24 hours.
No matter how weary or dreary
you may feel, you possess the certainty
that, during the day that lies before you,
absolutely anything may happen.

MONICA BALDWIN

Know how to do good a little at a time, and often.

BALTASAR GRACIAN

Don't be afraid to give your best to what seemingly are small jobs. Every time you conquer one it makes you that much stronger. If you do the little jobs well, the big ones will tend to take care of themselves.

DALE CARNEGIE

When a man realizes his littleness, his *greatness* can appear.

HERBERT GEORGE WELLS

No man is so poor as to have nothing worth giving. . . . Give what you have. To someone it may be better than you dare to think.

HENRY WADSWORTH LONGFELLOW

We can do no great things . . .
only small things with great love.

MOTHER TERESA

I always remember an epitaph which is in the cemetery
at Tombstone, Arizona. It says: "Here lies Jack Williams.
He done his damnedest." I think that is the greatest
epitaph a man can have—when he gives everything that
is in him to do the job he has before him. That is all you
can ask of him and that is what I have tried to do.

HARRY S. TRUMAN

*G*reatness is but
many small littles.

LATIN PROVERB

Whether our efforts are, or are not, favored by life,
let us be able to say, when we come near
to the great goal, "I have done what I could."

LOUIS PASTEUR

Determine that the thing can and shall
be done, and then we shall find the way.

ABRAHAM LINCOLN

You have got to have courage.

THEODORE ROOSEVELT

Nurture your mind
with great thoughts;
to believe in the heroic
makes heroes.

BENJAMIN DISRAELI

Nothing ventured, nothing gained.

ANONYMOUS

Take calculated risks. That is
quite different from being rash.

GEORGE S. PATTON

In great attempts,
it is glorious
even to fail.

CASSIUS LONGINUS

The fact is, that to do anything
in the world worth doing,
we must not stand back shivering
and thinking of the cold and danger,
but jump in and scramble through
as well as we can.

ROBERT CUSHING

Not knowing when

the dawn will come,

I open
every
door.

EMILY DICKINSON

Everyone is born a genius.

R. BUCKMINSTER FULLER

What you can do, or dream you can, *begin it;*
Boldness has genius, power and magic in it.

ANONYMOUS

Opportunity seldom knocks twice.

PROVERB

Now is no time to think of
what you do not have.
Think of what you can do
with what there is.

ERNEST HEMINGWAY

There is no security in this life.
There is only *opportunity*.

Douglas MacArthur

*A*sk, and
it shall be given you;
seek, and ye shall find;
knock, and it shall be
opened unto you.

Matthew 7:7

When one door closes, another door opens; but we
often look so long and so regretfully upon the closed
door that we do not see the ones which open for us.

Alexander Graham Bell

How many cares one loses when
one decides not to be something
but to *be someone*.

COCO CHANEL

f I accept you as you are,
I will make you worse;
however, if I treat you as
though you are what
you are capable of becoming,
I help you become that.

JOHANN WOLFGANG VON GOETHE

Remember always that you have not only the
right to be an individual; you have an
obligation to be one. You cannot make any
useful contribution in life unless you do this.

ELEANOR ROOSEVELT

To be what we are, and to become what we are capable of becoming, is the only end of life.

ROBERT LOUIS STEVENSON

Try not to become a man of success but rather to become a man of *value*.

ALBERT EINSTEIN

If you doubt you can accomplish something, then you can't accomplish it. You have to have confidence in your ability, and then be tough enough to follow through.

ROSALYNN CARTER

Be faithful to that which exists nowhere but in yourself— and thus make yourself indispensable.

ANDRÉ GIDE

I have had a long, long life full of troubles,
but there is one curious fact about them—
nine-tenths of them never happened.

ANDREW CARNEGIE

People are defeated in life not because of
lack of ability, but for lack of wholeheartedness.
They do not wholeheartedly expect to succeed.

NORMAN VINCENT PEALE

If a man will begin with certainties, he shall
end in doubts; but if he will be content to
begin with doubts, he shall end in certainties.

FRANCIS BACON

The only limit to our realization of tomorrow
will be our doubts of today.

FRANKLIN D. ROOSEVELT

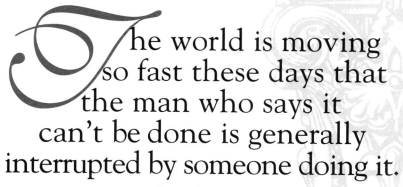

The world is moving so fast these days that the man who says it can't be done is generally interrupted by someone doing it.

ELBERT HUBBARD

If you really do put a small value upon yourself, rest assured that the world will not raise your price.

ANONYMOUS

Have you got a problem? Do what you can where you are with what you've got.

THEODORE ROOSEVELT

It is a mistake to try to look too far ahead. The chain of destiny can only be grasped one link at a time.

SIR WINSTON CHURCHILL

31

Aim for a star,

and keep your
sights high!

HELEN LOWRIE MARSHALL

Remember, you have to work.
Whether you handle a pick
or a pen, digging ditches
or editing a paper,
ringing an auction bell
or writing funny things—
you must work.
If you look around, you will see the
men who are the most able to
live the rest of their days without work
are the men who work the hardest.
So find out what you want to be, and
do, and take off your coat,
and make a dust in the world.

CHARLES READE

Always aim for achievement
and forget about success.

HELEN HAYES

34

There is always room at the top.

DANIEL WEBSTER

Hitch your wagon
to a star.

RALPH WALDO EMERSON

There may be more to learn
by climbing the same mountain a hundred times
than by climbing a hundred different mountains.

RICHARD NELSON

There have been others also
just as true and devoted to the cause—
I wish I could name every one—
but with such women consecrating their lives,
failure is impossible!

SUSAN B. ANTHONY

There is no such thing as a
great talent without great *willpower*.

HONORÉ DE BALZAC

*P*atience is a necessary
ingredient of genius.

BENJAMIN DISRAELI

It matters if you don't just give up.

STEPHEN HAWKING

Great works are performed not by strength,
but *perseverance*.

SAMUEL JOHNSON

Let me tell you the secret that has led me to my goal.
My strength lies solely in my *tenacity*.

LOUIS PASTEUR

Never give up and never give in.

HUBERT H. HUMPHREY

While there's life there's hope.

PROVERB

I am glad I am an optimist. The pessimist is half-licked before he starts.

THOMAS A. BUCKNER

An optimist sees an opportunity in every calamity;
a pessimist sees a calamity in every opportunity.

SIR WINSTON CHURCHILL

The purpose of life is to *believe,* to hope, and to strive.

INDIRA GANDHI

Every cloud has a silver lining.

PROVERB

Find a purpose in life so big it will challenge
every capacity to be at your *best*.

DAVID O. MCKAY

*L*ive up always
to the best and
highest you know.

HANNAH WHITALL SMITH

The roots of true achievement lie in the will
to become the best that you can become.

HAROLD TAYLOR

If you do the best you can,
you will find, nine times out of ten,
that you have done as well as
or better than anyone else.

WILLIAM FEATHER

Excellence is the best deterrent to racism or sexism.

OPRAH WINFREY

The *best* that an individual
can do is to concentrate
on what he or she can do,
in the course of a burning
effort to do it *better*.

ELIZABETH BOWEN

I don't want to make money, I just want to be *wonderful*.

MARILYN MONROE

A
single
sunbeam
is enough
to drive
away many

shadows.

SAINT FRANCIS OF ASSISI

Fall seven times, stand up eight.

JAPANESE PROVERB

I remember a very important lesson
that my father gave me
when I was twelve or thirteen.
He said, "You know, today I welded a perfect
seam and I signed my name to it." And I said,
"But, Daddy, no one's going to see it!"
And he said, "Yeah, but I know it's there."
So when I was working in kitchens,
I did good work.

TONI MORRISON

I don't want to express alienation.
It isn't what I feel. I'm interested in various kinds
of passionate engagement. All my work says
be serious, be passionate, wake up.

SUSAN SONTAG

Victory belongs to the most persevering.

NAPOLEON BONAPARTE

We are not interested in the possibility of defeat.

QUEEN VICTORIA

He conquers who endures.

PERSIUS

Don't make excuses— make good.

ELBERT HUBBARD

If you think you can win, you can win.
Faith is necessary to victory.

WILLIAM HAZLITT

We never do any thing well,
unless we love it for its own sake.

MARY WOLLSTONECRAFT

Work is and always has been my salvation and I thank the Lord for it.

LOUISA MAY ALCOTT

The key to whatever success I enjoy today is:
Don't ask. *Do*.

VIKKI CARR

You have to . . . learn the rules of the game.
And then you have to play it
better than anyone else.

DIANE FEINSTEIN

What you look for in the world, is not simply
for what you want to know,
but for more than you want to know,
and more than you can know.

EUDORA WELTY

The best thing in life is doing things
people say you can't do.

JENNIFER MOORE

The main thing is
to care. Care very hard,
even if it is only a game
you are playing.

BILLIE JEAN KING

The end crowneth the work.

ELIZABETH I

Nothing succeeds like success.

PROVERB

The secret of success is constancy to purpose.

BENJAMIN DISRAELI

Success is a . . . trendy word. Don't aim for success if you want it; just do what you love and it will come naturally.

DAVID FROST

Success consists of a series of little daily victories.

LADDIE F. HUTAR

Always bear in mind that
your own resolution to succeed
is more important than any one thing.
ABRAHAM LINCOLN

A great secret of
success is to
go through life as a man
who never gets used up.

ALBERT SCHWEITZER

If you wish success in life,
make *perseverance* your bosom friend,
experience your wise counselor,
caution your elder brother
and *hope* your guardian genius.

JOSEPH ADDISON

If you would hit the mark,
you must aim
a little above it.

Every arrow
that flies feels
the attraction
of earth.

Is there anything better
than to be longing for something,
when you know it is within reach?

GRETA GARBO

*W*hy not go out
on a limb?
Isn't that where the fruit is?

FRANK SCULLY

The ladder of success doesn't care who climbs it.

FRANK TYGER

Climb *high*
Climb *far*
Your goal the sky
Your aim the star.

INSCRIPTION ON HOPKINS MEMORIAL STEPS,
WILLIAMS COLLEGE

If you aspire to the highest place,
it is no disgrace to stop at the second,
or even the third, place.

CICERO

Hit the ball over the fence and
you can take your time
going around the bases.

JOHN W. RAPER

In the long run you hit only what you *aim at*.
Therefore, though you should fail immediately,
you had better aim at something high.

HENRY DAVID THOREAU

One can never
consent to creep
when one feels
an impulse to soar.

HELEN KELLER

Pay no attention to what the critics say;
no statue has ever been put up to a critic.

JEAN SIBELIUS

Make it a rule of life never to regret and
never to look back. Regret is an appalling waste
of energy; you can't build on it;
it's only good for wallowing in.

KATHERINE MANSFIELD

Keep away from people who try to belittle
your ambitions. Small people always do that,
but the really great make you feel that
you, too, can become great.

MARK TWAIN

Better three hours too soon,
than one minute too late.

WILLIAM SHAKESPEARE

You can overcome anything if you don't bellyache.

BERNARD M. BARUCH

There is nothing more potent than thought.
Deed follows word and word follows thought.

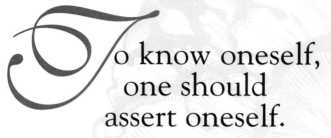

To know oneself,
one should
assert oneself.

If you have an important point to make,
don't try to be subtle or clever. Use a pile driver.
Hit the point once. Then come back and hit it again.
Then hit it a third time—a tremendous whack.

If a man can write a better book, or preach a better
sermon, or build a better mousetrap than his
neighbor, though he builds his house in the woods,
the world will make a beaten path to his door.

If a man does not keep pace
with his companions, perhaps it is
because he hears a different drummer.
Let him step to the music that he hears,
however measured or far away.

HENRY DAVID THOREAU

*E*very step is an end,
and every step
is a fresh beginning.

JOHANN WOLFGANG VON GOETHE

Keep adding, keep walking,
keep advancing: do not stop,
do not turn back, do not turn
from the straight road.

SAINT AUGUSTINE

Lives of great men all remind us
We can make our lives sublime.
And, departing, leave behind us
Footprints on the sands of time.

HENRY WADSWORTH LONGFELLOW

Cultivate your curiosity.
Keep it sharp and always working.
Consider curiosity your life preserver,
your willingness to try something new.
Second, enlarge your enthusiasm to include
the pursuit of excellence, following
every task through to completion.

JOHN W. HANLEY

If a job's worth doing, it's worth doing well.

PROVERB

Don't part with your illusions.

When they are gone you may still exist, but you have ceased to live.

MARK TWAIN

Deliberation is the work of many men.
Action, of one alone.

CHARLES DE GAULLE

Take time to deliberate, but when the time
for action has arrived, stop thinking and go in.

NAPOLEON BONAPARTE

*B*e not afraid
of greatness: some men
are born great, some
achieve greatness and
some have greatness
thrust upon them.

WILLIAM SHAKESPEARE

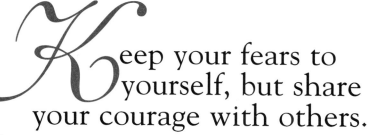

Keep your fears to yourself, but share your courage with others.

ROBERT LOUIS STEVENSON

Follow your honest convictions and be strong.

WILLIAM MAKEPEACE THACKERAY

Never run away from anything. Never!

SIR WINSTON CHURCHILL

The first thing to do in life is to do with purpose what one proposes to do.

PABLO CASALS

You will never "find" time for anything.
If you want time you must make it.

CHARLES BUXTON

I like a person who knows his own mind and
sticks to it; who sees at once what, in given
circumstances, is to be done, and does it.

WILLIAM HAZLITT

Work to me is a sacred thing.

MARGARET BOURKE-WHITE

Don't leave for tomorrow
what you can do today.

POOR RICHARD'S ALMANAC

Bite off more than you can chew, then chew it.
Plan more than you can do, then do it.

ANONYMOUS

You are richer for doing things.

JESSICA TANDY

One must learn by doing the thing, for though you think
you know it, you have no certainty until you try.

ARISTOTLE

Work and thou canst
not escape the reward....
The reward of a thing well
done is to have done it.

RALPH WALDO EMERSON

Determine never to be idle. . . . It is wonderful
how much may be done if we are always doing.

THOMAS JEFFERSON

First you have to learn something,
then you can go out and do it.

MIES VAN DER ROHE

Life is like a game of cards. The hand
that is dealt you represents determinism.
The way you play it is free will.

JAWAHARLAL NEHRU

*Destiny is not
a matter of chance,
it is a matter of choice;
it is not a thing to
be waited for, it is a thing
to be achieved.*

WILLIAM JENNINGS BRYANT

Making a success of the job at hand is the
best step toward the kind you want.

BERNARD M. BARUCH

The lure of the distant and difficult is
deceptive. The great opportunity is where you are.

JOHN BURROUGHS

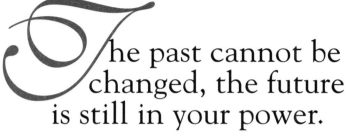he past cannot be
changed, the future
is still in your power.

HUGH WHITE

Make the best use of what is in your power,
and take the rest as it happens.

EPICTETUS

What we should do is not future ourselves so much.
We should now ourselves more.
"Now thyself" is more important than "Know thyself."
Listen, now is good.
Now is wonderful.

MEL BROOKS

*K*eep dreaming.

GEORGE FOREMAN

*T*he man who
has no imagination
has no wings.

MUHAMMAD ALI